a Pocketful
of Windows

*Poems to Gaze, Reach or
Crawl Through*

edited by Felix Hodcroft

VP

Valley Press

This pocketful is dedicated
to Martin and to Jenny
without whom
it wouldn't exist

First published in 2014 by Valley Press
Woodend, The Crescent, Scarborough, YO11 2PW
www.valleypressuk.com

First edition, second printing (February 2015)

ISBN 978-1-908853-40-0
Cat. no. VP0062

Printed and bound in Great Britain by
Imprint Digital, Upton Pyne, Exeter

www.valleypressuk.com/books/pocketfulofwindows

About the poetry in this book

It's sculpting words, ideas, emotions; to render fresh and almost transparent something just ... just out of reach.

It's getting inside your head, like an infection. It refuses to be forgotten; it wants to be passed on, and on.

It wrings the grey, and out streams colour. It's a double-shot espresso, a throatful of pure springwater.

It cuts to the core of the tangle that has no answer. Or sometimes it's inside drilling out. It's a window into someone else's soul, an escape-hatch out of yours.

Here's a pocketful of windows, to gaze, reach, leap, fly – or more often (being human) to crawl – through.

To find out who wrote what, when you want to, turn to pages 63-66.

Keep poetry in your pocket; to keep you.

Felix Hodcroft
Scarborough
September 2014

1. "gravity slips off me like a coat"

Camellia Sinensis

My kitchen faces east,
And in the first flush of dawn
I am at peace.
Early morning anoints my sacred space.
I unlock the tabernacle
And baptise with boiling water
dried, black, broken leaves.
Until they, and I, are born again.

My cup is china.
The tea from the flat lands of Assam.
By the miracle of monsoon
And the will of working women
I am provided the privilege of pleasure.
Silently, the camellia sinensis seeps into my soul.
Grace is given. Ritual and reverence exchanged.
In this moment, nothing else exists.

Teapot. Boiling water. Tea.
Three in one and one in three.
Teapot. Boiling water. Tea.
My blessed holy trinity.

Grace

I kneel alone in the wooden pew.
All is silent, still and calm.

Fingers of sunlight gently stroke
My shoulders, neck and cheeks.

Pulpit and choir stalls stand empty.
No sermon, hymn or psalm.

Never have I attended
Such a perfect service.

Under A Holderness Sky

The heat of the sun lifts water from pavements.
Steam rises, returning rain to piebald clouds.
The wheels of my car hiss through roadside ponds.
Wings of silver spray arch and fall. I am flying
under the vast Holderness sky, racing to the coast,
chasing grey clouds and banks of snow-white
mountains, above the sun-bright blue brilliance
and the shimmering glory of a double rainbow.

I Begin To See

A blackbird feeding
Brings me back to now.
Pain still grips,

But only in spasms
Receding, even for a moment,
I begin to see
The reflections
On the table top,
Such a mixture of muted colours
Interweaving,
Striking deep into the polished surface.

Carved In Stone

It might have been emblazoned on our arms,
embroidered on a sampler handed down,
or chanted as a mantra every day,
that *caveat* of 'What will people think?'

There always were imaginary folk
to sit in judgement of our every move
slightly off course, innovative or rash;
as kids, we never questioned who they were.

But now it's clear these phantoms don't exist
and didn't then; they were, like Santa Claus,
a lie – without the toys and tangerines –
a wicked ploy to keep us 'in our place'.

I've aged, of course, my scales fell long ago
and life's taught that those others just don't care
what kind of clown *I* am; it's *their own* show
concerns *them*, and *their* mantra: *laissez faire*.
Sad, this should come so late, but most I hate
my lack of chutzpah to participate.

Mr Wolf

The moon glares onto bitter snow
And looks for her prize.
She beams silent blue hues
To light his way.
It is freezing. Unquiet sleep
rattles the window as
The Werewolf locks himself
Inside his own cage.
She says, 'Come outside
And warm yourself by the Wolf's Sun.'
He turns and swallows the key.
'Who's afraid?' she asks, as if
Buttering toast. Then
Shakes the bars... 'Does
This make you angry?'

What's the time? Mr Wolf? What's the time?
Time is a mirror. Reflecting
Sound and heartbeat. Indifferent
To beauty and questions.
Teeth smile at what lies beneath;
And he sits marking time
With plastic forks
And horrible imaginings.
He samples the menu in his head.
Somebody in bed.
And the woodcutter mounts the stairs.

Breath begins to glow in the night.
And darkness gives in

To blue bright light.
The moon has no memory. In
Changing. Moving. It is now.
A growl.
Anger is bottled inside bars
And scratch marks crouch on the ceiling.
'It is coming,' he says, 'It is time.
It's irresistible. This fury.'

Visiting Time

'LIFT CALL' pressed, an arrow tings.
A patient on a trolley is manoeuvred out.
I step in. Doors slice me off from outside
as if they want to give me secret news.

Going up, but I'm weighed down.
Floors flash past the tiny window and ask:
How much of this might we find in you?
How much of this best not to know?

Is this my visiting time, or is time
visiting me? Perhaps the answer's here
where the lift aligns the chosen floor,
and gravity slips off me like a coat.

Arrows lead me to your bed.
From some deeper level you stir.
Eyelids flicker, then fall back asleep:
Like a lift coming, but going past.

amnesia

  i'll cliff jump
hit my head on a rock
  wave crash white noise
tick-tock tick-tock
  wake to the doctor's voice saying
'you must take this medicine,
you might not remember certain things,
like birthdays, or places you've been'
  i'll learn to ride a bicycle
have my first taste of sand and snow
  grow, strong
and forget, all about before.

Learning To Crawl

I smashed my head on life itself: affairs
and overtime turned me blue and black,
bureaucracy did my head in, addictions
left me gasping for a wholeness I could
not name. I railed and swore at bosses
and lovers who all turned away, shaking
their heads. I drove my car into a wall. An
ambulance took what was left of me, fed
me anaesthetic, placed me in bandages
and intensive care. An old man arrived
and held my hand. He said nothing but
stayed for weeks. The doctors said I

would not walk again. But the presence, beside me, one hand on mine, made me strong. Now, the nurses put the old man at one of end of the corridor, and me at the other. I crawl towards him, craving the kindness in his mouth and eye. It will take me years to reach him, and by the time I arrive, he'll be gone. By then, I'll know enough to sit next to some young sod, lying smashed up and ready to be healed.

Recovery

So you've pieced back
together your heart,
re-inserted those eyes
(that now see like a falcon)
and replaced the top of your skull.

Now take great gulps
of this incredible, fresh, new air;
blink into that
cauterising light
and laugh,
          laugh,
laugh out loud;

then start to *win*.

2. *"she is a song of so much possibility"*

Albert

The Norbreck Hotel, Scarborough, 1968

Poached from a paper round
to be a porter's assistant –
your assistant, weekends and holidays –
I worked there because you worked there.

Everybody loved you: small, skinny,
National Health specs; probably mid-fifties,
but to me, at fourteen, you were Methuselah.
And so funny! You'd slap a trailing leg to bring it in line,
or chase a pea around your plate, moaning
how hard life was – that even your vegetables
were giving you the runaround.

A Bradford man, you were football mad,
which explains why, four years later,
you turned up at Valley Parade to watch me play.
We met after the game: *You did all right lad...*
but then you would say that.
Then we lost touch. As you do.

Until today that is, when, walking down
memory lane past the hotel, I see you staring
owl-like through a window,
waiting for the coaches to arrive.

I Met A Woman Once With Violet Eyes

I met a woman once with violet eyes
Which had been her downfall. I looked in
Them then, saw the lost hopes, the tawdry lies
That men had told her, and the years of gin.
It had not been enough that special blue,
To bring her what she wanted, not at all.
If men really loved her she never knew,
Was it her eyes that caused each one to fall?
To be sure she was still pretty enough
At fifty-one, for many heads to turn,
A cut-price Cleopatra, who'd known it rough,
But could somehow make men want and yearn.
I saw violets today, growing by my front door,
So small, so shy, that blue. I thought of her.

velvet covered everything

I want that house
with the curvy seats
velvet covered everything
with mirrors and fires in
odd places.

I want that dressing gown
with cigar-cutter in pocket
velvet smooth sleeves
and thick velvet air
of 70s screen time.

I want that ice
and that bourbon
velvet throat gold
and the artsy twig woman
freckles like orange velvet.

Most of all
past the shady lamps
and the sighs in the looking glass
I want
that velvet moustache.

Christmas Truce 1972

Manzir and I ran the men's Trans-cultural ward.
Funny, when all I did was dish out curried mush
And sometimes give a 'thumbs up' sign, theek hay,
Similar to teeka, that in Urdu means injection.
A few days before Christmas Manzir had a plan.
'Rose, let's have things different, just this once.
More than turkey, snow-spray, us sitting in the office,
Wanting to be at home, if we have homes to go to?'
So in Handsworth, where methi scents the streets,
We drove to Manzir's uncle's darkened shop
And bought some crates of beer and many paan,
Yes we ate the usual turkey, snow-sprayed windows,
But on Christmas day we gave no medication at all.
Only betel nut and spice in broad green leaves.
Staff and patients sat close and quiet together,
Chewing that paan and spitting it out berry red.

Piano Girl

What Hell-land squeal is this –
this wrackling song she makes –
some slipped cog sprocketting loose –
the pressured pedal of her fate
that runs her wildly up and down
the unset fragments of her keyboard?

She is a song of so much possibility –
for there is consonance still
in the jagged sound waves I receive.
What experience is it that plays her
rough, that unreadies her and sours
and slams down these degenerate chords?

She is, of course, her own passion.
She has dumped too much of herself
in that double garage of life – lugged
things out from the house of her being:
But she knows the unwisdom of that,
until there is nothing left but slight.

How I would peel back the walls,
disperse the untuned wires of her rage
and search her with a chocolate look
melting smoothly into her morning
greeting her with a soft-touch song
to loose the ping-stretched fibres of her frame.

my time with rumi

for Chris Woodland

i went to the tavern last night and imagined i was a
    whirling dervish
i danced with men and i danced with god
i spun fun into drunken wouldbe lovers and then
whoever brought me there took me home.

on waking i watched the dawn
i listened for secrets and found them inside of me
    whispering
follow me follow me come to the field
and there you were lover
sat upon a leathery throne laughing
the elephant laughed too and my poetry shone
    through

i go about my day now
the glass blowers breath in my hands as i hold the
    food i can not eat
my mouth only hungry for my lover
a note tells of my need to close my eyes
and look with the other to see
the visitors who snuck in
a crowd of sorrows and malice who play upon this
    reed flute
whilst i sleep with my eyes open
your poetry my guide to my guides
i say welcome
to this being human

Learning To Dance

I gave my dancing shoes
to you.
You held them
tenderly
in your hand,
heels against your palm.

One day
you will fit them, warm,
to my feet
and you will teach me
the dance.
When it is finished,

the shoes will hold
the music
for me
so that my feet will remember,
should my mind,
undisciplined,
forget.

Travel Light

Now I must go
And empty my pockets
To lighten the load I carry,
So my travels will be light
Not held down by resentment and anger.

And why I am alive by skills
Unknown to me.
In pain, yes.
Bear it and live again;
The year is yet
To unfold.

Tracey Angel

What's the point in being an angel in today's world?

It was not what I expected
from a young woman standing at the corner of the bar,
a Breezer in one hand, a fag in the other.

She looked like all the rest,
smooth tanned skin between black t-shirt and black
    jeans' belt,
pink glittered lips, powder blue eyes.

It was the snake which caught my attention,
a coiled tattoo around her belly button –
it yawned, showing fangs,
before settling more comfortably
on its sun ripened nest.

I began with *Fancy a drink?*
And she started straight in with,
What's the point in being an angel these days?
No-one notices the miraculous.
No-one cares for the uncanny,
when all has to be understood and explained.

It's harder than you think to be celestial
in a world where mystery and magic are commodities.

I tried, *What's your name love?*
Hoping to prise her into my arms
before the next day dawned.

Tracey, she replied,
taking a slug of Bacardi, dragging on her cigarette.
She had the loveliest onyx eyes
and lips which I should have been kissing.
Instead her words kept on coming,

No-one searches for the ethereal,
bothers with the soul,
we all want happiness wrapped and tied with bows.
We're so distracted
by the constant boom of activity,
the interminable flicker of movement,
the unbearable chatter of information,
no-one listens for the sadness anymore.

I was losing patience,
even the thought of laying my aching head
where her snake slept
wouldn't hold me much longer.
Tell you what, I'll give you a package worth having,
darling,
and I laughed because it was funny.
She stared into my eyes,
hers were sparkling quartz,
Where's the sense in being an angel in today's world?

I was getting to the end of my tether,
You look like an angel to me, love,
so why don't you show a desperate man a miracle?

At which point her snake raised its head and
    beamed at me.
Ruby flames slipped from her pearly finger tips,
words branded in frost and burning oil
fell from her mouth,
It's colder than you think when you stop running
away from yourself,
which is why we all need central heating.
No-one wants the spaces in between.
Listen to the hush as the world weeps
and your spirit cries to be heard above the clatter
because joy is nothing without its opposite.
And her snake hissed.

Suddenly there was a bargy behind
and I was momentarily unbalanced,
when I looked up again
there was only the end of the bar,
a fag end in the ash-tray
and an empty Bacardi Breezer bottle.

Tracey, my angel,
was gone.

Bringing Lemons

I was sick

and you battled
an icy esplanade wind
and the flat's
steep green stairs
to bring me
from the supermarket
a bag of lemons

if I had been Rembrandt
I would have painted us both
at the open door
me in my blue dressing gown
you in your woolly grey hat

and later in the art books
we would have seen a detail
the darkness of the stairwell
the outstretched arms
across the threshold
lemons and hands
haloed in that interior light

Flea By Flea

Once a year
my father came home drunk.
No one ever told us why, but we knew.

We learnt things flea by flea.

How he'd lied about his age
and joined the Cavalry at sixteen.
Learnt to ride a horse in glorious manhood.

How he'd shivered in the trenches
picking fleas out of the seams of his great-coat.
How he'd slept in the mud and shaved in cold tea.

How he'd crawled over the top, head well down.
Times when he'd dragged friends back to safety
got the lucky ones off to field hospital.
How once he'd been among the lucky ones
dragged off to sleep between sheets, wounds dressed –
not all the shrapnel removed, but most of it.

How he'd written to my mother to send him a nutmeg.
Years later she learned why. The men passed it round to
    suck
before thermometer time, to boost their temperature into
another day of bliss.

But there were no more stories. Four years of lice-ridden
memories smouldered, buried deep, erupting once a
    year, stirred
by the ritual of the Annual Reunion of the Cavalry
    Regiment.

3. "I want you to love you"

Excuses. Excuses.

He plots in the early dawn
I can't go to school Mum
My head aches
I feel sick
Don't make me go.

He rehearses as the day breaks
I can't go to school Mum
I've lost my P.E. kit
I haven't done my homework
Don't make me go.

He pleads over breakfast
I can't go to school Mum
My stomach hurts
You don't understand
Don't make me go.

As she turns away annoyed,
he whispers …
They'll be waiting for me.

Breakage

Hard on the outside
Soft on the inside
As I look down

You break my leg
And soft stuff oozes out.
Even the hard stuff
Just snapped.

It Was They Who Made You Feel This Way

Someone has made you feel like this, Hate
It's all you breathe, not for them but for you
The accident you had, the mistake you made
They hated you for it, the venom in their eyes

Dirty, Insignificant, Unwanted, Useless,
Who are you? What are you? Worthless!
It wasn't your fault but that look hurt nevertheless
The blind panic inside yourself. Hurry! A fake smile
    will do,

I need someone, You need someone...
Hold me, Hug me, Love me, Breathe me.
Touch me. Only platonically,
A friend ... Grounded innocence.

You are beautiful, You are smart, You are kind...
No! No! No! Finger over lips. Cover up the naughty
    words,
Lies! ... No, Truths ... I want you to love you and
    your mind.
These words are not dirty. They are you. They are
    divine.

Throw off those shackles, Unlock that door! GO!

It was they who made you feel like this, to hate
    themselves
A little more. I love you. You love you.
It was they who did the wrong.

Wallis Simpson Said

Aged 8, and the girl
sat next to her says
'Do you really think you
should be wearing that?
It's a bit tight isn't it?'
and though it's her favourite
she hides it away
never wears it again.

At 10 someone says
'You're still eating crisps'
and though it had never occurred
to her not to
she doesn't again, throws them
in a rubbish bin on the
way home.

Aged 11 and average
in class yet if you
asked her the calorie value
of anything she'd come top
no problem.

13, and her best friend says
she's discovered this

fantastic new diet – you can
eat anything you want
anything at all
but
you just have to make yourself sick
afterwards.

Excitedly
they discuss the
best way to do it –
she's heard you should drink
salt water beforehand
someone else says long fingernails are best...

They'd probably agree that
you can't be
too rich
but there's no question that
you can never be
too thin.

When A Snowman Melts

You might think that when a snowman melts
someone has died.
But they haven't.

Instead, someone has warmed and begun to flow,
said sorry for being such a frozen lump,
realised they are part of everything,
and started to cry.

Orange

Orange is a colour dazzling
In its brightness. You smell
Rather than see it, taste its sticky
Sweetness.

Wear it if you dare – in its glare
All else will be dimmed into
Drab insignificance by your
Magnificence.

In a garden you hear it
Singing among the flowers
Hitting all the high notes in wild
Jubilation.

But it excels itself at harvest
With moon huge and glorious
Filling the sky with its enormous
Extravagance.

Prometheus

It was the lightning that did it;
That rent the grey, staff-room curtains

And caused the poor sod to glimpse it:
The bowl of apples kept up there,

Ruddy and gleaming like fire;
That lured him seven flights of stairs,

Past the porter's loo, and higher
Than any other boy in school –

Then down, down with his bright burden
Burning his trembling fists, and out

In stealth onto the sodden field,
To spill the stuff and split the loot:

A bosom-full of burnished fruit
Ripe to fatten his bosom friends.

Perhaps he did it to be cool,
Be hero-like, or take the piss;

Now the pride and fortune are his –
At least until break is finished,

When the teachers shall give him hell.
His muddy feet have marked the floors

And lesser, famished friends will tell;
In any case, CCTVs

Perch like eagles above the doors:
They shall pluck his liver for this.

Stones

In my left hand trouser pocket,
(Along with hanky and worry beads)
I carry two stones.
Pebbles picked from a Corsican shore.
One smooth, the other rough.
Reminders of the two sides of life.

But here's the strange rub of the thing.
As the years pass
The rough stone is becoming smoother
And the smooth stone rougher.

Hatching

I will tell you how it is...
after an eternity
of incubation, barely
conscious,
comes the time.

Months of mining,
mole blind,
an impenetrable wall
with a tiny hammer,
eventually
makes a hole.

You take a single sip
of fresh air, and
become aware of
the impossibility of
your situation.

Trapped
in a womb tomb
tired, tied, now
you must turn and
turn and

persistent

pick and chip to make
a manhole cover:
a trap-door which,
if pushed hard enough,
(and I mean really hard!)

will pop
open
and
with a final,
almighty
struggle, you

flop,

damp and exhausted,
into the possibility of tomorrow.

4. *"walking in on the ceiling the world all upside-down"*

Porth Oer

On the headland I lean
into the westerly wind,
taking the angle of the
terse scrub at the edge.

There is a vault in the gorse;
the entrance, a dark pupil,
the iris edged by a knotwork
of white sheep fleece;

barrel-roofed with
spiny truss and rib,
floored with grass, still
holding the impress

of lambs and ewe.
I can see myself,
maybe six or seven,
crawling through;

moving from light to
vitreous semi-darkness
to squat down,
fetal and tight

in the oily earth smell,
the pulse of sea breaking

on the beach below.
Stalled now on my walk

I look at this boy: grey
shorts, knitted pullover,
scuffed shoes, checked
shirt – one collar tucked in,

one out; curled, knees
drawn up, like an ancient
burial awaiting discovery.
I would extend a hand, say

'Come on! Leave this squint
view, walk with me'; but the boy
is a relict, should not
be excavated. Besides,

my track now is up from
Porth Oer towards Mynydd Carreg,
the sunlight warming the tops,
sufficient to melt a stone.

Three Cranes Lane

Men with keys, sticky beer, masonry,
bird shit, broken glass –
same old, same old.

And from the sewer:
lapis lazuli, counters, signet stones,
thin spoons for powders.

Abandoned Buildings

Abandoned buildings
In the middle of fields
Seem to say
'I am free and I don't need you.'

They were told of their freedom
By the little flowers that break their way through
In places no man meant them to be.
And then the wind and the wild came
Alongside the little flowers.
It came and said, 'Come back to me.'

At first the building argued
And stood true to its form,
And said, 'I am strong this way,
I was made this way, this is what I am'.
But the wind and the wild insists,
'This is not who you are. Come back to me.'

For a while it is dangerous.
Caught between form and wild.
But piece by piece the form becomes free,
And the sky breaks through
Til the sun reaches its long lost places,
And nestles there in patches of tenderness.

The building begins to sigh more often,
And remember how once it came from somewhere
    else.
It wants the sun to kiss it where it had once been kissed
And feel the rain pour over it where it had once felt
    rain

And feel the freedom of things that grow;
Things that flower, and seed,
And scurry, and flap, and bleed.

A man may want to rescue it with scaffolding
Or a bulldozer
But he is already too late.
It has known itself
And it is free.

My Beautiful City

Raining all day but
at evening a breeze-broom sweeps the clouds into a
    corner,
the sun's eye opens wider and wider,
the sun's tongue licks the rinsed streets dry
and the sun's breath blesses us as
we drink air rich and clean as cream.

And we are children
comforted by forgiveness after punishment,
reassured that today didn't matter and's
almost over and tomorrow's a tablet of fresh clear
    paper
that longs for us to write on it
This is my story – Now it begins!

Breath Of God

Poised on the tip
of the hand of a clock
between now
and now.

Slip down the hand of time
through air and water.
To the floor of the ocean.

Feel fish tickle feet,
silken fronds of seaweed
stroke limbs and body.

Held firmly in the embrace of water
look up unharmed
through filtered light
into the eye of the sun.

Climb the ladder of light
through fish and weed and water
through the surface,
out into the air of my own home,
walking in on the ceiling
the world all upside-down,
tops of polished furniture glowing
among ledges piled high
with dust of years.

I am the dust
floating like a feather
on the breath of God,

a single speck among ten thousand
dancing into the ray of the sun
light reflecting, golden, glorious.

Glorious.

Reborn

Outside,
    Muted thrashing, shouting,
    Echoing hollow sounds
    That ring around the edges.
    Inside,
    Embryonic stillness embraces
    the kiss of a turning point
    Between life and death.
    Hands
    Above the water
    In sinuous spiral, waving,
    Even clutching, slowly clenching.
    Body
    Below the surface
    Sensing the water-world
    Where dreams weave in refracted light
    Until
    hands grab, hook,
    haul you like a fish
    Into the rough bottom of a boat.
    Reborn,
    Out of time and place,
    You breathe the air
    But your soul swims with dreams and fishes.

Night Dive

Confusion. Noise.
Racing for slack water,
clumsy in our rubber armour,
weighed down with lead,
we roll into the water with a splash.

Suddenly, the quality of sound changes,
the cacophony gone.
Now we are surrounded
solely by the sound
of our own exhalations.

The Sea, The Sea.
Back in the comfort of her cold embrace,
weightless in the inky blackness,
I am at peace.

Down here even you are an angel,
your body wreathed in a halo of light,
your breath rising towards me;
the bubbles coruscating
with an emerald green phosphorescence.

Forty metres down.
Torches on.
Ready for touchdown in
Inner Space.

Puffs of white sand rise beneath us.
Glints of silver.

Our searchlights cut through the dark,
pick out the rusting hulk of the wreck,
on the edge of vision.

You set off to hunt for brass,
for the ship's bell.
I hunt for bryozoans,
the alien life of this artificial reef.

Our air is low.
Time to ascend,
to float free in
Nothingness.
Hard even to know up
from down.
Frighteningly liberating.

Then we break through
that glass ceiling.
Back to the surface,
back to people,
back to relationships,

to the pain
of the 'real' world.

to the drudgery of ordinary existence.

The Green Field

I dreamed I was a horse
and the green field all around me
kissed my feet.
In my eyes two doves smiled
and the sun and moon were mine
in equal measure.
The day was music within my bones.
The night was music within my blood
and I was blessed.

And blessed
I ran within that green field, where,
in its sweetest, farthest corner I saw
lay buried, a silver-box – so small,
yet within the box,
lay the root, the tree,
the waiting forest of my dreams.

And from this, I ran.
And ran, and ran, far far from it, until –
at last, I saw it no more –
and was sad.
For years I ran and ran and ran – until –
the moon it was that stopped me. Under her light,
I looked down and saw that
within my own body lay that green field,
within my own heart lay that silver box.
Still and silent – in the moon's light.

Waiting.

5. *"clocks broke; time froze"*

Born

I heard the sound of that crack
before I felt the pain of it.
When I looked I saw it;
barely beating my heart
was there in his hands,
wet with my blood, new born
and his eyes beheld it as such.

I was still afraid
but too tired now
to entertain fear's demands,

we were silent together for the longest time.

Lilitu

Fallen angel in search of a home.
sucking the lifeblood
from vulnerable men in sleep.

Awaken, poor vulnerable man
to aching erection and weakness of spirit.
Call it the sign of her coming, not yours.

The troubled dreams of a believer
turned infidel, held in thrall by the
sweet parted lips of Lilitu.

Cherry Pie

for James Nash

I've always wanted to eat cherry pie –
your cherry pie, so succulent and rich,
with its lacquered lids and soft bathing fruits
brimming out of your buttery cups.
I will always want to eat cherry pie –
your cherry pie, the one you serve nightly
to those you simply love,
at your doting board, tuckered and starched.
I dream of eating cherry pie.
Sweaty, yearning, caught in twisted sheets,
I suck on the sugared berries, too sweet,
then the bittered after-taste bites.
For cherry pie, your cherry pie,
is forbidden nectar, never mine.

Your Skin Is Cool

Your skin is cool and and soft and smells of you,
When I wake to the pricking of night fear.
You sleep, and are quite oblivious to,
The rocks and shoals through which I steer.
We're on different journeys through this night,
I am awake and you sail far away,
Though your body is close and I hold it tight,
You may not stir until the birdsong day.

'Til then I have your breath to listen to,
Can inhale your sweet and precious scent,
And warmed by being so close to you,
May sleep again, with all my terrors spent.
We float on this raft together, we touch,
And on this long voyage take turns on watch.

A Room For You

When sleep takes me through doors I have locked,
to dry rot, mice droppings and moth-eaten linen,
I try to prepare a room for you to come home to.
I can't find clean sheets, dustpan or brush.
The floor boards break under my feet

and I fall and I fall into that sudden awakening
and a thirst on me for ice-cold water.
The resounding thrum of your absence
drives me from my bed to stand at the window
and watch the garden grow out of moon-dust.

There was such a light the night I lay with you
in the field when the white owl floated over us.
I will leave my bed tonight, lock the door on
rooms full of your absence and find you again
in the garden, growing out of moon-dust.

middle names

he took matchbox-size pieces
of me
replaced them with memories
of using each others' toothbrushes
holding hands through tube rushes
hiding in anderson shelters constructed from sheets
'cause the world was falling all around us
and weeks past
fast, like trains
slow, like hands creeping gingerly into coat pockets
and together we built
a love made to last.

Kate

The splashing is a seagull
cooling and smiling
in the pond

and the grass is warm
and a whipped cream cloud
rolls passively
across the purest sky you've ever seen

and there is no rush.

I breathe in and I wonder if
I've ever seen anything as beautiful as this

and yes, I have.

Scientific Observations Of Love

Love
approached me
the way the apple
approached Isaac Newton:
I did not see love coming.
Instant and intense.
It rushed
and gave me a headache.

You sank into my life
the way Archimedes
sank into his bath:
everything else overflowed.
Work, friends, sleep.
Only you remained,
and filled every corner of my life.

We broke rules;
breaking speed limits,
you were too busy
looking at me
to look at traffic lights.
I was too high from falling.

In love,
time did not bother us.
Clocks broke; time froze.
We were wonderfully
alone there.

And the future was persistent:
splitting us apart
the way Rutherford split the atom.
We cannot be fused back together.

I have been approached
by love
since you.
But it has never been the
Eureka! moment

like our time.

Custom

for Olive, on our 65th Wedding Anniversary

See a cat claim the comfiest cushion,
the kingfisher his observation perch,
note also where the same mare's teeth
chamfer again her chosen stretch
of the paddock gate's top rail,
how boldly the gold Helianthus
outstares the gaze of the sun
and how these words speak left to right

but when, for the twentythousandth time,
you hear my '...love you, too',
that's simply because it's true.

6. *"I stand at the gateway to that life, your guardian"*

11.57pm 28th September 1986

Silver blade slices
glints in the overhead light
cutting into your darkness.
Your pool where you swum
and the thump, thump sound have gone.
You cry
as you must
and live.

Evening

He pauses at the children's doors,
listens for the air slipping
backwards and forwards in their lungs.
It comforts him. Downstairs, they talk.
She tells him if he needs deodorant, says
she is bothered about the ironing.
The washing up leans beneath drips.
At night, sometimes, he can't sleep
for fear of what may come into the world,
a terrible cloud, a vast and vicious raven,
spreading across the globe, shouting his name
so loud it defeats his own heartbeat.
'This world bothers me,' he tells her. 'The kids.'
'Sweetheart,' she says.
They hold each other before sleep.

Four Horsemen

My mother fought long to subdue that subtle
    virulence;
With her birth-pangs and gift of her body fluids
She gave me early my full inheritance,
Struggled to last out to my second
Birthday.
                But it didn't really work, that didn't.

My mother fled away down the long dust tracks
When the riot of warriors suddenly erupted,
They severed her neck with three quick hacks
As she held me to her body, in her final
Protection.
                But it didn't really work, that didn't.

My mother came along to my Primary School
When I was starting out in Year 4, I remember.
She would bring that familiar syringe full
Of its wild beast juices to keep us
Happy.
                But it didn't really work, that didn't.

My mother offered me her drought-withered nipples,
Cracked and hard, trying to sustain me.
Walked twenty-three miles to the clinic packed
With a throng of mothers, for the chance of a
Miracle.
                But it didn't really work, that didn't.

My father always worked abroad to earn our bread,
And brought back more than cash for my waiting
    mother.
She took the antivirals and made off, once he was
    dead;
Left me in a cot at the Kids' Home,
Rocking.
                Sure seemed to work, that did.

My father took me over to the '06 World Cup,
Heaved me on his shoulders in the massing crowds.
I helped with the war-cry, when the bastards turned
    up:
'I'd rather be a Paki than a Kraut,' were the
Words.
                Sure seemed to work, that did.

My father could be quite a laddie in his beers,
Smashed mum, us kids, and the house when he
    chose.
But I went one better, and I waited for the queers,
Pissed blind with the lads, rampaging
Wild.
                Sure seemed to work, that did.

My father used to mould me in the famine of his
    thought,
Of his care and interest, friendship and protection.
Over all the years, I remember, he taught
me how to let the rest of the world be
Buggered.
                Sure seemed to work, that did.

Sleeping Child

You sleep, while names of villages rise
and fall away, tail-lights dwindling ahead
until only we summon the sign
for crossing deer, steer by the constellation
of a pub. The edges where the wipers
shove the rain gel and tremble, sucked thin
by small riptides. I rest my elbow on
the door-frame like my father would and read
the road through fingertips. A milestone
unfolds, lets go of the verge, the barn owl
gone before I realise – that's how we get home.
And what will you recall of the sudden lift
from car to bed, your eyes broken open
for a moment by the light in the hall?

Day

This is for the mothers
whose kids weren't there when they woke this
    morning,
who dressed without any unusual interruptions,
whose coffee wasn't carried upstairs,
who made themselves breakfast.

This is for the mothers
who arranged their coping mechanisms
instead of flowers,
who made space on the window ledge to see the
    world outside
and counted their chickens, not cards.

This is for the mothers
who took the long haul down the stairs
with their third load of washing
and wondered if they would make the bottom
without an audible sob.

This is for the mothers
who didn't eat lunch,
who took some fresh air on the back doorstep
with a cup of tea and questioned
every decision they had ever made.

This is for the mothers
who were not defined by sentiment
nor bolstered by company
nor bewildered by annual exceptions
nor faced with only those faces that can be all
the questions and all the answers in every
moment of expression.

This is for the mothers
whose kids weren't there when they woke this
    morning
and yet
they were mothers
still.

Thirteen

Where are you my little girl?
Lost for ever,
glimpsed between the storms and uncertainness,
the child you were,
the woman you are becoming.

Who are you my little girl?
your own woman,
fighting against boundaries,
so much more peaceful for me
to remove the constraints.

What are you my little girl?
Butterfly-like
your wings beat against protection,
your spirit needs to soar,
freedom beckons.
Life.
I stand at the gateway to that life,
your guardian.

When are you my little girl?
Always.

The Light Of You

In the dreamtime before waking,
I lived again a winter afternoon

alone with you; the light fading
from the window, a coal fire,
the smell of baking bread,
the child I was listening as you
sang to music playing on the radio.

You twirled and clapped your hands.
I sat on the kitchen floor, flexing
my toes to the rhythm of your dance.
When the music stopped, my infant
voice called you to squat beside me.

Your smile crinkled lines round your eyes.
The light of you touched me.
I had no words to tell you this.

You stroked my hair, touched your lips
to my head. I butted into your warmth,
nuzzled into the smell of you.
You lifted me. Desire made me whimper
until my mouth filled with the flesh of you.
You wiped away my dribble.

Today you move your hand to the rhythm
of my voice singing the songs of your youth.
I stroke your hair, touch my lips to your head.
You whimper your need. I hold a drinking cup
to your mouth and wipe away your dribble.

Your smile crinkles lines round your eyes.
The light of you touches me.
I tell you this.

Kitchen Sink Painting

I look through the kitchen door
into a scullery. I've been there before.
Time scarred walls in a cold out-house,
where caseinpainted walls blister
into sepia lines brushed through
a requisitioned cream and green existence.

I hear the *whoomph* of the gas being lit,
making steam as the stream
of hot water hits the sides
of the deep ceramic sink.
Cheaper to fill than the tin bath,
and him clean as a wink in no time.

A soft gas light glows through
from the kitchen, I taste smoke in air
warmed by clinkers from the old black range.
Using the softest of the kitchen cloths
she rubs him down,
rinses away grated soap suds.

His spindled legs are held tense
until the water warms them.
He stands firm, right hand grasping her pinny,
his left held away from his body to balance,
fist clenched, to concentrate
on the new perspective, being so high.

She finds the warmed towel, to wrap this scrap,
her little man, holds him close to her body.

In The Bathroom

The night of my Mum's funeral
I sat in her cosy pink bathroom
listening to the piercing screams
of one creature killing another.

Perhaps a fluffy innocent rabbit
like the soft toy in the den next door
having its liver ripped out
by a fox or a yellow eyed stoat

Or perhaps a disease ridden rat
crawling along the bank of the leat
and getting its just deserts
from next door's friendly, slobbery dog.

Through the open window I could taste
warm night air. Moths kamikazed in
to butt themselves against the light
then, stunned, quivered in basin and bath.

The cries grew quieter, the slaughter over.
I cradled my mug of tea, glad
to have heard death so heartily
enacted. This the given order,

Survival of the fittest. Nothing
I could do about it. You can't stop
Mother Nature having her wicked way.
Closing the window, I went back to bed.

The Wet Gabardine

Too many coats
are housed
in the darkness of my understairs cupboard.

Flecked wool and fleece
caress
my face. Fake furs beckon me further forward.

Fumbling blindly
I brush
against the shroud of a sombre gabardine.

And I inhale
the scent
of the long dead, forlorn ache of fatherhood.

Tentatively,
with the
reverence of a priest preparing for mass

I kiss the soft
fabric.
My arms stealing into the depths of the sleeves.

And fastening
the buttons
with my father's military precision

I step outside.
Soft June
rain on the upturned collar, the epaulettes

releases from
the coat
the pungent aura of my father's being.

Rain permeates
the cloth
and conjures my father into the present

as if he were
scented
lotus flower petals opening in tea

by the power
of warm
June rain with its heavenly vitality.

But he has crossed
beyond
earthly continents, and no Skype or email

wandering the
ether
can reconnect us like this wet gabardine.

7. "fly fly fly
to those outstretched arms"

That's What I Remember

My daughter danced at your wedding
a tiny red rosebud clinging
to your willowing stems.
Her dad was your best man.
Serious about the job
he bought a book on etiquette
but forgot to do his flies up.
I spooned salty soup, listening
to flat Norfolk vowels vie with
lilting Irish cadences.

There followed more births,
Christenings and parties,
a divorce (mine)
lost babies (yours)
all the things that mesh
two family patterns
over thirty years.
Tricky recalling
the when and the wheres.

Students in seventies Hull,
the four of us must have known
there would be funerals.
We just never imagined our own.

My daughter danced at your wedding
and I'm so glad that we were there.

Despite

Despite the harmonica's squeaky tune
That sends the ballerina thumping across
The unsprung stage.

Despite the golden glitter of the ice cream seller
Who sells dripping 99's to the passers by
As they flake out along the sea front.

Despite the impotent tongue's fear to stick out and lick
Tears from cheeks, returning to swallow some more
Until all sorrow is drunk.

Despite Rufty Tufty's annoying bouncing around
The high hedged maze before spilling out into the
Fifty pence arcade.

Despite the fifty pence arcade once being penny arcade
Until inflation inflated the bouncy castle leaving it
Untouched by children's feet.

Despite children untouched by human hands for fear of
Touching, left only to seek comfort on bouncy castles
Too expensive to enjoy.

Despite the honk of horns and quick vicars squelching
On about death and disgrace, but who cares for dying
When the day is sunny.

Despite all that, despite all that and more:
Due to some infectious desire for life and living
Tomorrow has not been cancelled.

The Old Pig

He was old, you told me.
The pig I now imagine, hanging sweet as a bag of
    sugar out in the barn.
Your job was always to feed him – and him
licking your hand as if it were pressed silk.
So many times, you told me the story.
Your guts turning, churning – knowing his future.
Brushing the long crease of your skirt –
watching him eat. Fat, contented.
Turning the iron handle of the sty door –
a kind jailor you must have seemed.
The sky above the door – blue as your eyes.
And the straw in his heart – stiff with fright on that
    last day.
Both of you willing that day not to come, but
    knowing it would.
Your face turned away to the sky –
love and anguish mixed with mud – a bloody
    cocktail.
Every ambush requires that there are two.
Your hand on the door, closing it.
The old pig, listening for your voice, found only
    silence.
Turn his face to the sky you tell the men.
You replay the ambush many times through all the
    years.
Because the pig forgives you.
Endlessly.
Even, as they bring the knife towards him.
He forgives you.

Heron

You wouldn't be surprised if you heard
the clanking of metal when he took off.

Perhaps you've wandered into Jurassic Park?
Ridiculous, this gangling oddball.

But not that skewer of a beak
you imagine a fish seeing

through the shattering glass,
the whirl of water.

The Minutes

In the morning fresh minutes are waiting.
Hundreds crowd your bed, litter the floor.
There are so many, threading

down the stairs and out the door.
In the evening, as the sky darkens,
you look for the minutes but most

have gone. As you watch, another
vanishes. The phone rings.
Two minutes go.

In bed, you close your eyes
and ask for more.

Rehearsal

Life's not a rehearsal, someone says (everyone,
    probably) yet
on this hot afternoon, on our cramped and patched
    back lawn,
I'm sucking a teddy-shaped orange ice-cube for yes –
we have a freeze-tray now, 'Cold!' and I
spit it out into your hand and, as
quick as a flash, your hand stuffs it down under my
viyella collar and 'Mummy! That's not funny! Stop!'
I squeal, kissing you,

hating this, hating this,
raising the cup to your crusted Sahara lips, this
time you manage a few drops and 'Cold!' you gasp,
'Cold!', something not quite a smile ripples over your
    starving,
bone-face as I kiss you I kiss you I kiss you.
My whole life rehearsing for this.

Pebbles In My Pocket

At times hardly knowing I've got them:
miniature speckled eggs, hiding
in the seams with flecks of fluff
to be rolled lightly between fingers,
flicked aside, forgotten.

Other times they're a monstrous size,
huge unwieldy rocks whose weight makes
misshapen material split.

Touching their roughness, my fingers bleed.
They are veined with my years.

I try to sew my pockets up
but stitches unravel faster
than I can possibly go.
Some days I can skim stones on water
some days I cannot walk.

An Offer

To be taken by the hand
To the fairytale.
To witches and wonderment.
Darkness and light.
A place where dreams
Are made
With nightmare figures, foes.

The beast has big eyes
And the bears will be home for
Breakfast.
Apples poison
And needles prick my fingers. But,

I believe in magic
And the lies of the woodcutter.
I shall go to the ball and
The beanstalk will break the giant.
I am protected.
My hand is held and I am with him.

Trapeze

The clowns are leaving the ring
With squirts and somersaults.
In the wings your hands
Touch gently and your eyes
Meet in a whispered smile,
Loud and fast the band
Plays for your entrance.
The rope ladders fall.
Cat-like you climb lithely up
Higher and yet higher
To the crown of the tent.
You've no idea what it feels like
To be the focus of a thousand eyes.

Whatever you do now, don't look down.

The lights are dimming.
For a millisecond your whole life
Passes before you
As the drums roll.

Then grab the bar and fly, fly, fly
To those outstretched arms

And trust, trust, trust.

Notes on the poems

page 4. **Camellia Sinensis** is by **Sue Wilson**. See also p. 54.

p. 5. **Grace** is by **Chris Woodland**. Chris' collection *The Creative Spirit* was self-published in 2007; he died in 2011. See also pp. 20 & 62.

p. 5. **Under A Holderness Sky** is by **Norah Hanson**, from her collection of the same name (Valley Press, 2013). See also pp. 41 & 50.

p. 5. **I Begin To See** is by **Helen Prince.** Helen died in 2014. See also p. 16.

p. 6. **Carved In Stone** is by **Maurice Rutherford.** Maurice's selected poems, *And Saturday Is Christmas* is published by Shoestring Press (2011). See also p. 44.

p. 7. **Mr Wolf** is by **Jeanette Hambidge**. See also pages 22, 32 & 61.

p. 8. **Visiting Time** is by **Stuart Larner.** See also p. 25.

p. 9. **amnesia** is by **Olivia Walker**. See also p. 42.

p. 9. **Learning To Crawl** is by **Miles Salter**, from his collection *Animals*, published by Valley Press (2013). VP also publishes his collection *The Border* (2011). See also pp. 45 & 59.

p. 10. **Recovery** is by **Mike Di Placido**, from his collection *A Sixty-Watt Las Vegas*, published by Valley Press (2013). Smith/Doorstep published his *Theatre of Dreams* (2009). See also pp. 11 & 59.

p. 11. **Albert** is by **Mike Di Placido**, from his collection *A Sixty-Watt Las Vegas*. See also pp. 10 & 59.

p. 12. **I Met A Woman Once With Violet Eyes** is by **James Nash**, from his collection *Some Things Matter: 63 Sonnets* (Valley Press, 2012). See also p. 40.

p. 12. **velvet covered everything** is by **Barrie Hardwick**. See also p. 42.

p. 13. **Christmas Truce 1972** is by **Rosie Larner**.

p. 34. **Breath Of God** is by **Joyce Bell**. See also pp. 21 & 26.

p. 35. **Reborn** is by Tony Howson, from his collection *The Crow Road to Eden* (Valley Press, 2012). See also p. 57.

p. 36. **Night Dive** is by **Paul Hughes**.

p. 38. **The Green Field** is by **Helen Burke**, from her collection *The Ruby Slippers* (Valley Press, 2011). It was first published in *Dream Catcher*. See also p. 58.

p. 39. **Born** is by **Ele Lawlor**. See also p. 15.

p. 39. **Lilitu** is by **Helen Barter**.

p. 40. **Cherry Pie** is by **Kate Evans**. See also p. 17.

p. 40. **Your Skin Is Cool** is by **James Nash**, from his collection *Some Things Matter: 63 Sonnets*. See also p. 12.

p. 41. **A Room For You** is by **Norah Hanson**, from her collection *Under a Holderness Sky*. See also pp. 5 & 50.

p. 42. **middle names** is by **Olivia Walker**. See also p. 9.

p. 42. **Kate** is by **Barrie Hardwick**. See also p. 12.

p. 43. **Scientific Observations Of Love** is by **Rachel Glass**.

p. 44. **Custom** is by **Maurice Rutherford**. See also p. 6.

p. 45. **11.57pm 28th September 1986** is by **Lesley Ince**. See also p. 50 – same child, thirteen years later!

p. 45. **Evening** is by **Miles Salter**, from his collection *Animals*. See also pp. 9 and 59.

p. 46. **Four Horsemen** is by **Nigel Gerrans**, from his collection *Tenebrae* (Valley Press, 2009). A volume of selected poems, *It Is I Who Speak*, is forthcoming from VP in 2015.

p. 48. **Sleeping Child** is by **John Wedgwood Clarke**, from his collection *Ghost Pot* (Valley Press, 2013). See also p. 31.

p. 48. **Day** is by **Philippa Blakey**.

p. 50. **Thirteen** is by **Lesley Ince**. See also p. 45.

p. 50. **The Light Of You** is by **Norah Hanson,** from her collection *Love Letters and Children's Drawings* (Valley Press, 2011). See also pp. 5, 41.

p. 52. **Kitchen Sink Painting** is by **Jo Reed,** from her forthcoming collection *Life Class* (Valley Press, 2015). VP also publishes her collection *Stone Venus* (2011).

p. 53. **In the Bathroom** is by **Sue Wilsea.** See also pp. 56 & 60.

p. 54. **The Wet Gabardine** is by **Sue Wilson.** See also p. 4.

p. 56. **That's What I Remember** is by **Sue Wilsea.** See also pp. 53 & 60.

p. 57. **Despite** is by **Tony Howson.** See also p. 35.

p. 58. **The Old Pig** is by **Helen Burke,** from her collection *Here's Looking At You Kid* (Valley Press, 2014). See also p. 38.

p. 59. **Heron** is by **Mike Di Placido,** from his collection *A Sixty-Watt Las Vegas.* See also pp. 10 & 11.

p. 59. **Minutes** is by **Miles Salter,** from his collection *Animals.* See also pp. 9 & 45.

p. 60. **Rehearsal** is by **Felix Hodcroft.** See also p. 33.

p. 60. **Pebbles In My Pocket** is by **Sue Wilsea.** See also pp. 53 & 56.

p. 61. **An Offer** is by **Jeanette Hambidge.** See also pp. 7, 22 & 32.

p. 62. **Trapeze** is by **Chris Woodland.** See also pp. 5 & 20.